Discover Planets

Discover Jupiter

Margaret J. Goldstein

Lerner Publications ◆ Minneapolis

Lerner Publications Company
A division of Lerner Publishing Group, Inc.
241 First Avenue North
Minneapolis, MN 55401 USA

For reading levels and more information, look up this title at www.lernerbooks.com.

Main body text set in Adrianna Regular 14/20.
Typeface provided by Chank.

Library of Congress Cataloging-in-Publication Data

Names: Goldstein, Margaret J., author.
Title: Discover Jupiter / Margaret J. Goldstein.
Description: Minneapolis : Lerner Publications, [2018] | Series: Searchlight books. Discover planets | Audience: Ages 8-11. | Audience: Grades 4 to 6. | Includes bibliographical references and index.
Identifiers: LCCN 2017046681 (print) | LCCN 2017051672 (ebook) | ISBN 9781541525429 (eb pdf) | ISBN 9781541523357 (lb : alk. paper) | ISBN 9781541527850 (pb : alk. paper)
Subjects: LCSH: Jupiter (Planet)—Juvenile literature. | Space sciences—Juvenile literature.
Classification: LCC QB661 (ebook) | LCC QB661 .G655 2018 (print) | DDC 523.45—dc23

LC record available at https://lccn.loc.gov/2017046681

Manufactured in the United States of America
2-47019-34667-12/20/2018

Contents

Chapter 1

KING OF THE PLANETS

More than two thousand years ago in ancient Rome, people looked into the sky at night. They wanted to understand the universe. They saw lights shining in the darkness. These lights were stars and planets. One light looked bigger and brighter than the others.

Jupiter looks like a bright light in the night sky.

Jupiter is about 88,846 miles (142,984 km) across at its widest point. Earth is about 7,926 miles (12,756 km) across.

The Romans named it after the king of their gods, Jupiter. Jupiter was the god of light and the sky.

Jupiter is the largest planet in our solar system. It is bigger than all the other planets combined. Jupiter is so big that thirteen hundred Earths could fit inside it!

Hangers-On

A moon is a large object that orbits a planet. Four big moons orbit Jupiter. They are called Ganymede, Callisto, Io, and Europa. Many smaller moons also orbit the planet. Scientists have counted more than sixty of them.

Rings orbit Jupiter too. These rings are flat disks made of dust and tiny pieces of rock. They are thin and hard to see. Small moons sit between Jupiter's rings. These moons and rings travel around Jupiter.

In 2017 the spacecraft *Juno* captured this image of the edge of Jupiter and two of its moons, Europa (*left*) and Io.

STEM Highlight

The spacecraft *Voyager 1* and *Voyager 2* studied Jupiter's largest moons in 1979. Scientists learned a lot about the moons from these spacecraft.

Io has many volcanoes. Callisto is pitted with craters. Europa is covered with a thick crust of ice. Scientists think a deep ocean lies beneath the ice.

Ganymede is the largest moon in our solar system. It is bigger than Mercury, the smallest planet. In 1995 the spacecraft *Galileo* visited Ganymede and found a magnetic field around the moon. Ganymede is the only moon scientist know of that has its own magnetic field.

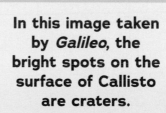

In this image taken by *Galileo*, the bright spots on the surface of Callisto are craters.

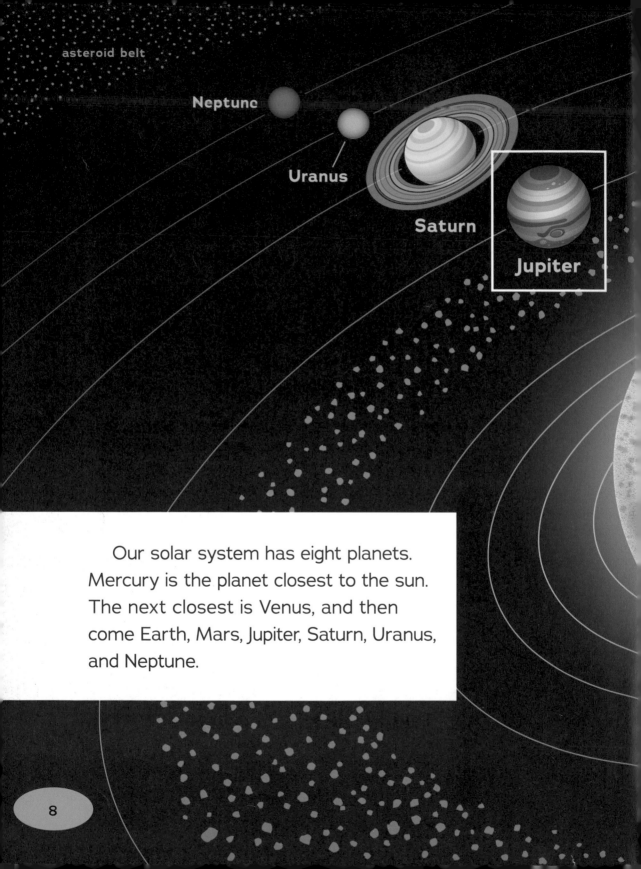

asteroid belt

Neptune

Uranus

Saturn

Jupiter

Our solar system has eight planets. Mercury is the planet closest to the sun. The next closest is Venus, and then come Earth, Mars, Jupiter, Saturn, Uranus, and Neptune.

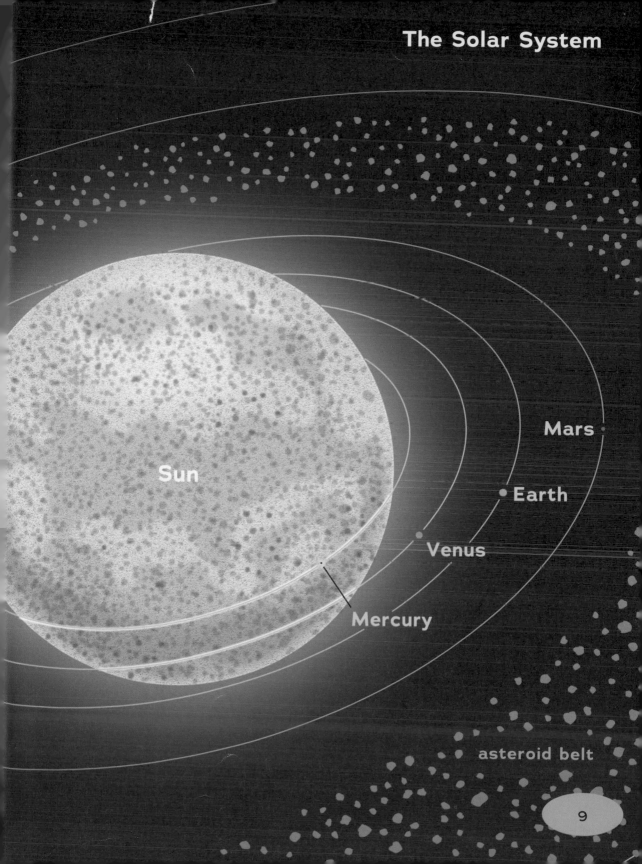

The Solar System

Sun

Mercury

Venus

Earth

Mars

asteroid belt

9

As Jupiter spins, part of the planet faces away from the sun. This part of the planet is very dark.

On the Move

All the planets in our solar system orbit the sun. A year is the time it takes for a planet to travel once around the sun. One year on Earth takes 365 days. One year on Jupiter takes 11.86 Earth years.

Jupiter spins too. A day is the time it takes for a planet to make one full spin. A day on Earth lasts twenty-four hours. A day on Jupiter lasts nine hours and fifty-five minutes. Jupiter spins faster than any other planet.

Chapter 2

GAS GIANT

If you flew a spacecraft to Jupiter, you'd have nowhere to land. Jupiter doesn't have any solid ground. It doesn't have a rocky surface like Earth. Instead, it is made of gases, including helium and hydrogen. Saturn, Uranus, and Neptune are also big balls of gas. Scientists call these planets gas giants.

Jupiter is made up of gases, just like stars are. Some scientists think that if Jupiter were even bigger, it would be a star instead of a planet.

Stormy Weather

Jupiter's atmosphere is filled with thick, colorful clouds. Light and dark clouds make a striped pattern. The stripes are called zones and belts. Zones are areas of whitish clouds. In zones, winds blow from west to east. Belts are areas of reddish-brown clouds. In belts, winds blow from east to west.

Jupiter is also stormy. Bright bolts of lightning flash through the clouds. Strong winds blow. These winds can reach 400 miles (644 km) per hour.

A powerful telescope took this image of Jupiter, which shows its stormy surface and the zones and belts.

The biggest storm on Jupiter is called the Great Red Spot. It is bigger than Earth. No one knows when the storm began. Many researchers believe British scientist Robert Hooke first saw it through a telescope in 1664. So it might be at least 350 years old.

A camera on the spacecraft *Juno* took this photo of the Great Red Spot in 2017. The photo shows the Great Red Spot's true colors.

STEM Highlight

Comets are icy bodies that travel through a solar system. In 1993 astronomers Eugene and Carolyn Shoemaker and David Levy studied photographs taken with a powerful telescope. The photos showed a comet orbiting Jupiter. Jupiter's powerful gravity had broken it into pieces. The broken comet was headed for a crash with Jupiter.

For six days in July 1994, pieces of the comet hit Jupiter. Scientists on Earth watched. This was the first time they had observed a collision between objects in space. It helped scientists study how other collisions in space have changed the solar system.

A scientist created this image by putting together several photos of the comet hitting Jupiter in 1994. When pieces of the comet hit Jupiter, scientists saw bright flashes of light.

Interior Department

Underneath Jupiter's stormy atmosphere is a thick layer of liquid hydrogen and helium. Beneath that is an even thicker layer of liquid metallic hydrogen. This hot, soupy substance creates Jupiter's magnetic field and electricity. Scientists don't know what the very center of Jupiter is like. It might be a hot ball of rock and metal.

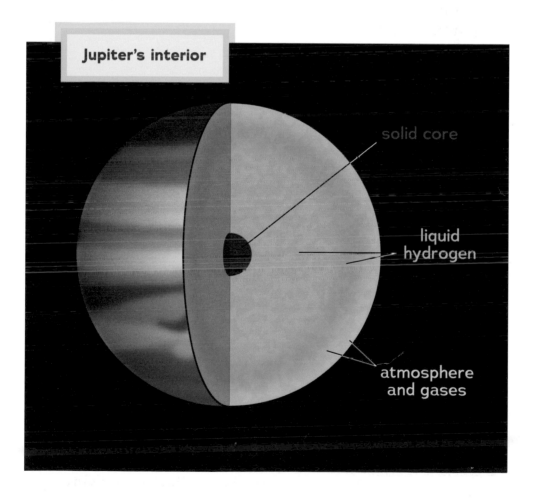

Jupiter's interior

solid core

liquid hydrogen

atmosphere and gases

Voyager 1 **took this close-up image of Jupiter's cold, stormy surface.**

At the top of its clouds, Jupiter is extremely cold. Temperatures there can be as low as -260°F (-162°C). The deeper you go inside Jupiter, the hotter it becomes. The core might be more than 35,000°F (19,427°C). That's hotter than the surface of the sun!

Chapter 3

LOOKING UP

Ancient sky watchers didn't have telescopes. With just their eyes, they saw Mercury, Venus, Mars, Jupiter, and Saturn at night. They didn't see Neptune or Uranus. These planets are too far away.

Jupiter (*left*) and Venus are the two brightest planets that we can see in the night sky.

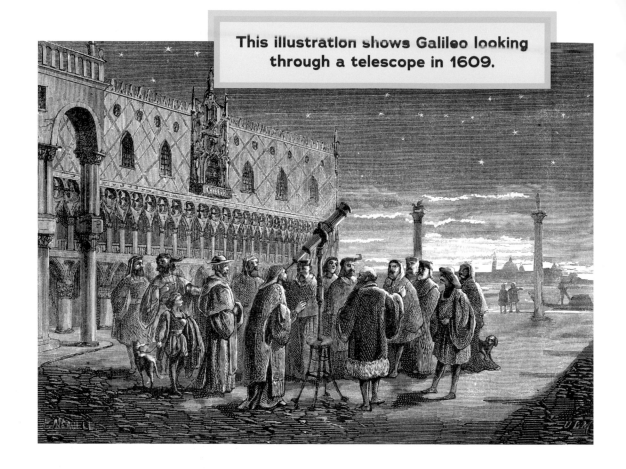

This illustration shows Galileo looking through a telescope in 1609.

With the naked eye, Jupiter looks like a small golden light at night. But with a telescope, you can see the planet's striped atmosphere, its big moons, and the Great Red Spot. In 1610 the telescope was a brand-new invention. That year Italian astronomer Galileo Galilei looked at Jupiter with a telescope. He saw its four biggest moons: Io, Europa, Ganymede, and Callisto. He watched them each night for a week. He saw that they orbited Jupiter.

Eyes on the Sky

After Galileo, other astronomers watched Jupiter through their telescopes. In the late seventeenth century, Italian astronomer Giovanni Cassini studied Jupiter's moons, clouds, and the Great Red Spot. He recorded their movements. By studying these movements, he was able to estimate how quickly the planet was spinning.

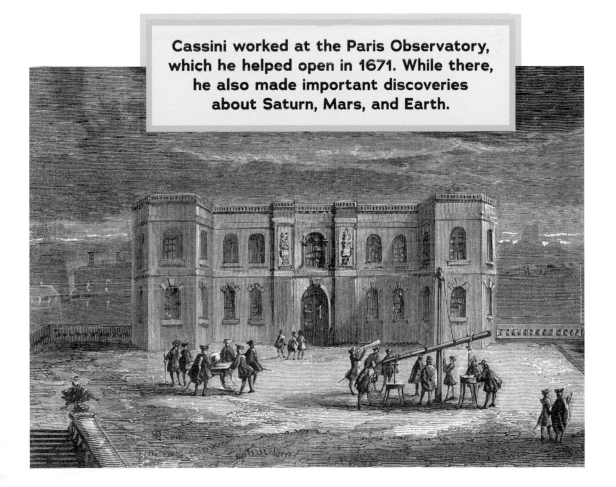

Cassini worked at the Paris Observatory, which he helped open in 1671. While there, he also made important discoveries about Saturn, Mars, and Earth.

The first radio telescopes were built in the 1930s. Scientists used this radio telescope to measure radiation from the sun.

In the twentieth century, engineers built bigger, more powerful telescopes. They also built radio telescopes. These devices detect waves of energy called radiation. Using a radio telescope in 1955, US astronomers Kenneth Franklin and Bernard Burke detected radiation coming from Jupiter. The planet's magnetic field produced the radiation.

STEM Highlight

Auroras are displays of colored light that are visible in the nighttime sky. Auroras occur on Earth near the North Pole and South Pole. The light comes from electrically charged particles moving along Earth's magnetic field and colliding with other particles in Earth's atmosphere.

Auroras take place on Jupiter too (*pictured*). They are much bigger and brighter than auroras on Earth. This may be because of the strength of Jupiter's magnetic field and the speed that the planet spins.

Blast Off

Many space vehicles have visited Jupiter. The vehicles have sent photographs and information back to scientists on Earth.

The spacecraft *Pioneer 10* flew past Jupiter on December 3, 1973. *Pioneer 11* flew past on December 2, 1974. The two spacecraft carried cameras. They carried telescopes and instruments that measured light and radiation. As they flew by Jupiter, they gathered data about its atmosphere and magnetic field.

An artist created this image of *Pioneer 10* flying over Jupiter.

Astronauts launched *Galileo* from the *Atlantis* space shuttle while orbiting Earth. *Galileo* then took six years to reach Jupiter.

In 1979 *Voyagers 1* and *2* made close-up investigations of Jupiter's moons. They photographed the Great Red Spot. They also discovered Jupiter's rings.

The *Galileo* spacecraft reached Jupiter in 1995. One section of *Galileo* left the main craft and dove down through Jupiter's clouds. On the way down, the vehicle analyzed Jupiter's gases and weather systems. *Galileo*'s main craft orbited Jupiter for eight years. The craft studied Io's volcanoes, found Ganymede's magnetic field, and found evidence of a water ocean on Europa.

Chapter 4

MISSION TO JUPITER

A spacecraft called *Juno* left Earth in August 2011 and arrived at Jupiter in July 2016. Then it began to orbit the planet. *Juno* carried eight instruments for studying the planet. These instruments measured light and radiation coming from Jupiter. They also studied Jupiter's gravity and magnetic field.

This illustration shows *Juno* in orbit. Scientists made *Juno*'s wings from solar panels so the craft could get power from the sun.

This image was taken by JunoCam. The colors were changed to make Jupiter's stripes easier to see.

A camera called JunoCam took close-up pictures of the Great Red Spot and other parts of Jupiter. It took the first pictures of the north and south poles of the planet. The US National Aeronautics and Space Administration (NASA), which runs the US space program, let people on Earth take part in JunoCam's mission. People could help decide which parts of Jupiter the camera photographed. When the pictures came back to Earth, people could view and make changes to the photos using their own computers.

Discovery

In its first year orbiting Jupiter, *Juno* made exciting discoveries. It found clusters of cyclones at Jupiter's north and south poles. The giant spinning storms are hundreds of miles across.

Juno even recorded whooshing noises coming from Jupiter's auroras. The sounds are too high-pitched for human ears. Machines lowered the pitch so humans could hear them. The sounds come from waves of radiation. By studying them, scientists will learn more about Jupiter's auroras.

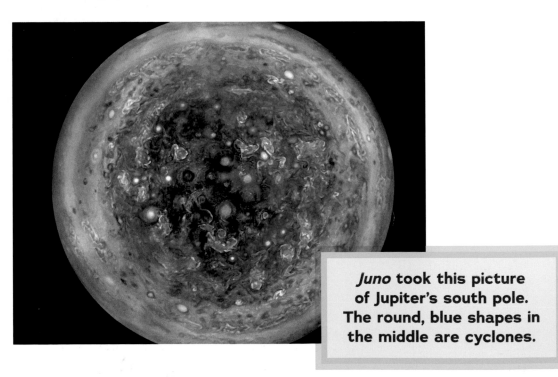

Juno took this picture of Jupiter's south pole. The round, blue shapes in the middle are cyclones.

An artist's image shows *Juno* flying over Jupiter's north pole.

Mission Accomplished

Scientists planned for *Juno* to orbit Jupiter twelve times. Then, at the end of the mission, they planned to send *Juno* to burn up in Jupiter's atmosphere. This way, the spacecraft wouldn't crash into Jupiter's moons and cause damage. Thanks to *Juno*, scientists know more than ever about Jupiter. But there is still much more to find out!

STEM Highlight

Scientists think that life depends on three ingredients: liquid water, elements such as carbon and hydrogen, and energy. All three together can cause chemical reactions that form life. The ocean water on Europa (*pictured*) might be suited for life. The elements might be in the rocky ground beneath the ocean. And volcanoes and hot water might provide the energy to start chemical reactions. NASA plans to send a spacecraft called *Europa Clipper* in the 2020s to study whether life has already formed on Europa.

Looking Ahead

Jupiter is still full of unanswered questions. Scientists are working to find out more about the planet. Here are just a few of Jupiter's mysteries. Maybe one day you'll be the one to solve them!

- Is there life in the ocean on Europa? What will *Europa Clipper* find when it reaches Jupiter's big moon?

- How old is the Great Red Spot? It has been spinning for hundreds of years. Could it be even older? Pictures from JunoCam might tell us more about the big storm.

- Jupiter's auroras are about one hundred times brighter than auroras on Earth. What makes them so bright? Data from *Juno* might solve the mystery.

Glossary

astronomer: a person who studies objects and forces outside Earth's atmosphere, such as planets, stars, and energy traveling through space

atmosphere: a layer of gases surrounding a planet, a moon, or another object in space

aurora: a display of colored lights in the nighttime sky. Auroras appear when electrically charged particles hit a magnetic field.

estimate: to give or form a general idea about something

gravity: a force that pulls objects in space toward one another. Jupiter's gravity pulls objects toward the planet.

magnetic field: a region around a planet or another object that gives off a force called magnetism. Magnetism pulls on some kinds of metal.

orbit: to travel around another object in an oval or circular path

radiation: energy that takes the form of waves or particles

solar system: a group consisting of a star and the planets and other objects that orbit the star. In our solar system, the star is called the sun.

telescope: an instrument that makes distant objects look bigger

volcano: an opening in the surface of a planet or moon through which hot rock, metal, or gases sometimes gush out

Learn More about Jupiter

Books

Chiger, Arielle, and Matthew Elkin. *20 Fun Facts about Gas Giants*. New York: Gareth Stevens, 2015. Take a trip to the outer solar system to explore the gas giants: Jupiter, Saturn, Uranus, and Neptune. This book will be your guide.

Squire, Ann O. *Planet Jupiter*. New York: Children's Press, 2014. Find out more about how Jupiter was discovered and what scientists know about the planet.

Zuchora-Walske, Christine. *We're the Center of the Universe! Science's Biggest Mistakes about Astronomy and Physics*. Minneapolis: Lerner Publications, 2015. In ancient times, astronomers thought everything in the universe circled around Earth. That turned out to be wrong. This book examines changing scientific beliefs.

Websites

Our Universe
https://www.esa.int/esaKIDSen/OurUniverse.html
The European Space Agency hosts this website, which includes sections on the sun, planets and moons, stars and galaxies, comets and meteors, and the entire universe.

Solar System 101
https://solarsystem.nasa.gov/kids/index.cfm
This NASA website lets you explore the sun, planets, moons, and other objects in our solar system. The site also includes games, puzzles, and other activities.

What Is a Planet?
http://kids.nationalgeographic.com/explore/space/what-is-a-planet/#planetary-lineup.jpg
This site from *National Geographic Kids* includes fun facts and pictures, with information about each planet and much more.

Index

Photo Acknowledgments

The images in this book are used with the permission of: Cooldyx/Shutterstock.com, p. 4; NASA/JPL, pp. 5, 7, 14, 16, 22, 23, 25; NASA/JPL-Caltech/SwRI/MSSS/Roman Tkachenko, p. 6; © Laura Westlund/Independent Picture Service, pp. 8–9, 15; NASA/JPL-Caltech/SwRI/MSSS/ Gerald Eichstadt/Sean Doran, p. 10; NASA/JPL-Caltech/SwRI/MSSS/Gerald Eichstaedt/John Rogers, p. 11; NASA/ESA/A. Simon (GSFC), p. 12; NASA/JPL-Caltech/SwRI/MSSS/Bjorn Jonsson, p. 13; Viktar Malyshchyts/Shutterstock.com, p. 17; Universal History Archive/Getty Images, p. 18; Oxford Science Archive/Print Collector/Getty Images, p. 19; Underwood Archives/Getty Images, p. 20; NASA/ESA/J. Nichols (University of Leicester), p. 21; NASA/JPL-Caltech, pp. 24, 27; NASA/ JPL-Caltech/SwRI/MSSS/Betsy Asher Hall/Gervasio Robles, p. 26; NASA/JPL-Caltech/SETI Institute, p. 28.

Front cover: NASA/JPL-Caltech/SwRI/MSSS/Gerald Eichstadt/Sean Doran.